INTRODUCTION

Welcome back to FastTrack®!

Hope you enjoyed *Bass 2* and are ready to play some hits. Have you and your friends formed a band? Or do you feel like soloing with the recording? Either way, make sure you're turned up loud…it's time to jam!

As always, don't try to bite off more than you can chew. If your fingers hurt, take some time off. If you get frustrated, put down your bass, relax and just listen to the song. If you forget a technique, rhythm, or note position, go back and learn it. If you're doing fine, think about finding an agent.

CONTENTS

ABOUT THE AUDIO

Again, you get audio tracks with the book! Each song in the book is included, so you can hear how it sounds and play along when you're ready.

Each audio example is preceded by one measure of "clicks" to indicate the tempo and meter. Pan right to hear the bass part emphasized. Pan left to hear the accompaniment emphasized.

> To access audio visit:
> **www.halleonard.com/mylibrary**
>
> Enter Code
> **5343-6124-6879-0331**

7777 W. BLUEMOUND RD. P.O. BOX 13819 MILWAUKEE, WI 53213

Visit Hal Leonard Online at
www.halleonard.com

LEARN SOMETHING NEW EACH DAY

We know you're eager to play, but first we need to explain a few new things. We'll make it brief—only one page...

Melody and Lyrics

There's that extra musical staff again! Remember, this additional staff (on top) shows you the song's melody and lyrics. This way, you can follow along more easily as you play your accompaniment part, whether you're playing, resting or showing off with a solo . . . well, sometimes bass players do get a solo.

And if you happen to be playing with a singer, this new staff is their part.

Endings

In case you've forgotten some of the **ending symbols** from Songbook 1, here's a reminder:

1st and 2nd Endings

These are indicated by brackets and numbers:

Simply play the song through to the first ending, then repeat back to the first repeat sign, or beginning of the song (whichever is the case). Play through the song again, but skip the first ending and play the second ending.

D.S. al Coda

When you see these words, go back and repeat from this symbol: 𝄋

Play until you see the words "To Coda" then skip to the Coda, indicated by this symbol: ⊕

Now just finish the song.

That's about it! Enjoy the music...

Back in the U.S.S.R.

Words and Music by John Lennon and Paul McCartney

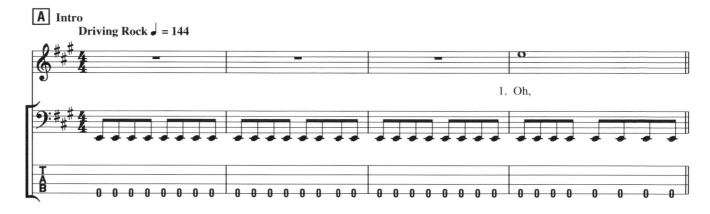

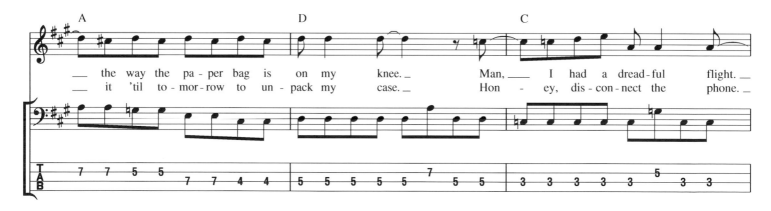

Back in the U. S. S. R. ___

Back in the U. S.

back in the U. S. back in the U. S. S. R. ___

Well, the

D Bridge

D7

A7

U-krane girls real-ly knock me out. _ They leave the _ west be-hind. _ And

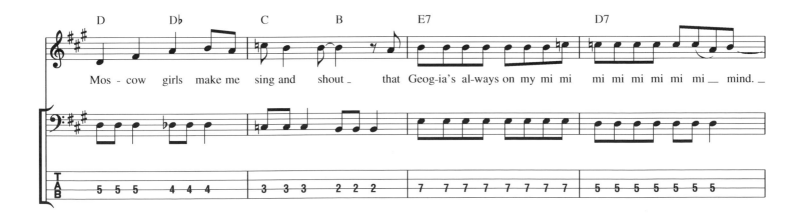

D   Db   C   B   E7   D7

Mos-cow girls make me sing and shout _ that Geog-ia's al-ways on my mi mi mi mi mi mi mi mi _ mind. _

4

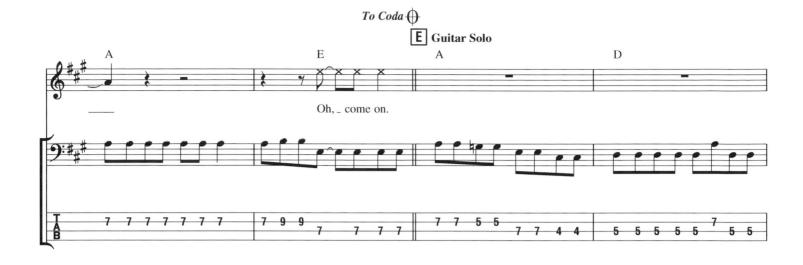

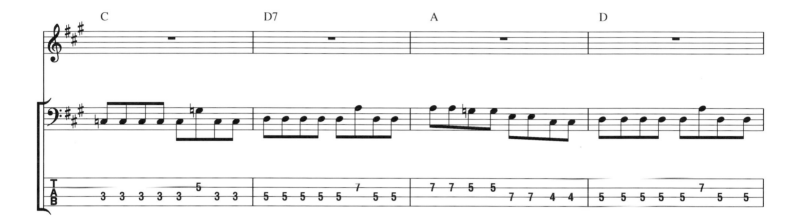

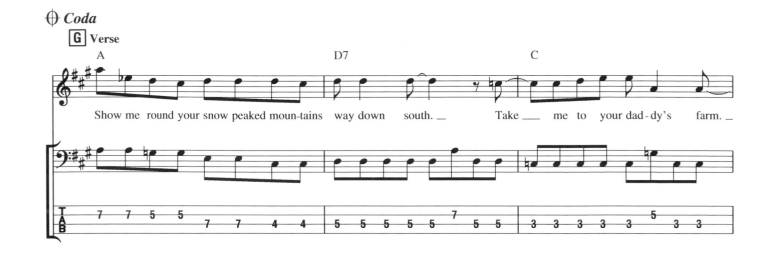

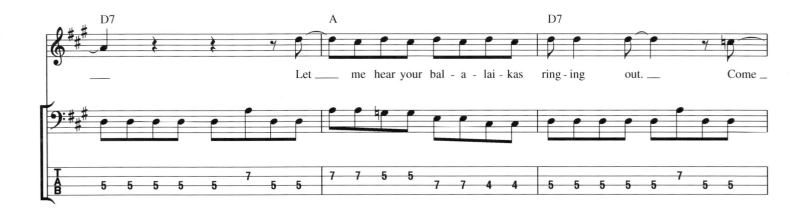

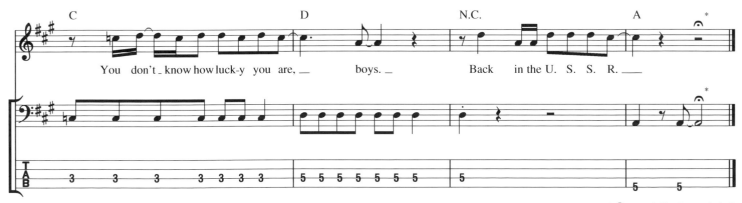

* ⌒ means hold as long as desired.

Born to Be Wild

Words and Music by Mars Bonfire

Yeah, dar-lin' gon-na make it hap-pen. Take the world in a

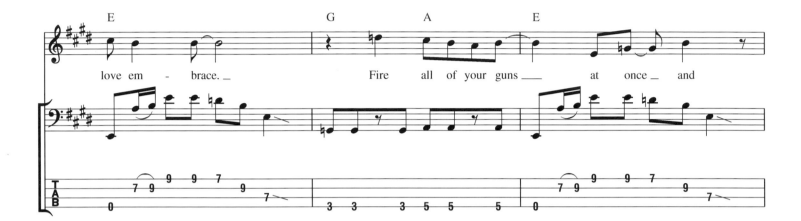

love em - brace. _____ Fire all of your guns _____ at once _____ and

ex - plode in - to space. _____ _____ Like a true na - ture's child _____

we were born, born to be wild. _____ We can climb so high. _____

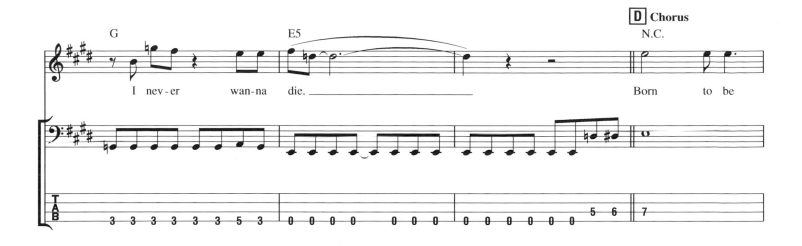

D **Chorus**

I nev-er wan-na die. _____ Born to be

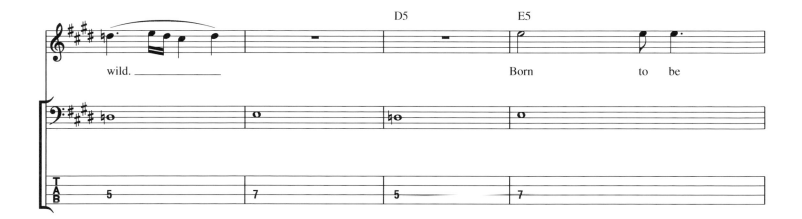

wild. _____ Born to be

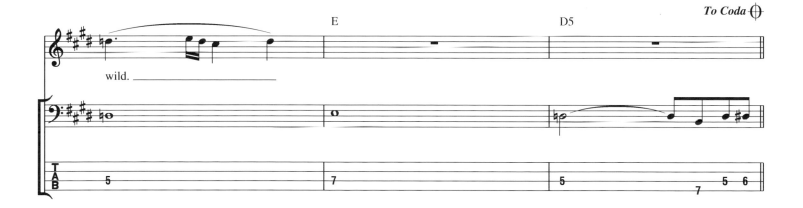

To Coda ⊕

wild. _____

E **Organ Solo**

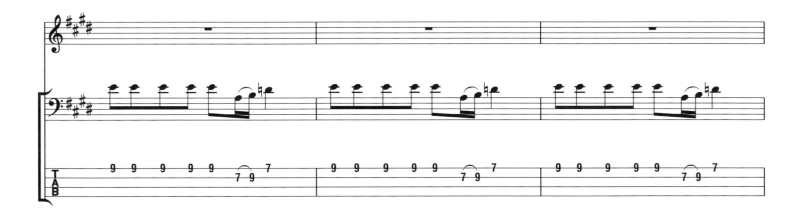

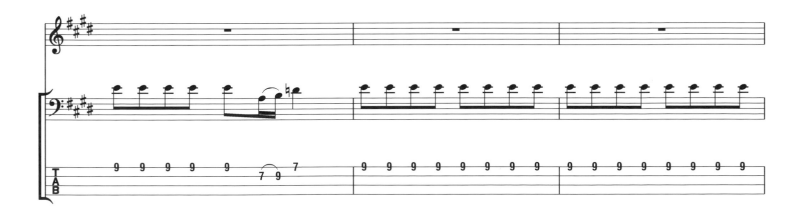

D.S. al Coda
(take 2nd ending)

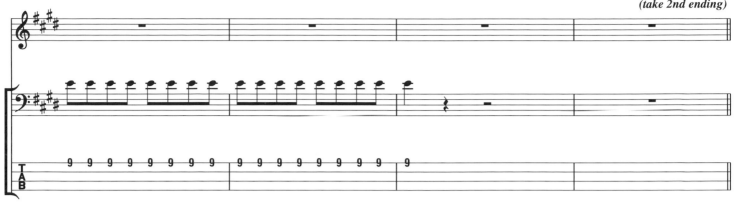

Coda

F Outro

E5

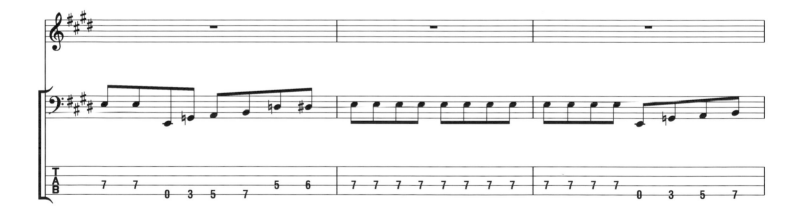

I'm Your Hoochie Coochie Man

Words and Music by Willie Dixon

C Chorus

what this all a-bout. I'm here. _____
Hoo - chie Coo - chie man. I'm here. _____
don't you mess with me. I'm here. _____

Ev - 'ry-bod-y knows _ I'm

here.

I'm the Hoo - chie Coo-chie man. _

1., 2.

Ev - 'ry-bod-y knows _ I'm here.

2. I

3.

Ev - 'ry-bod-y knows _ I'm here.

Imagine

Words and Music by John Lennon

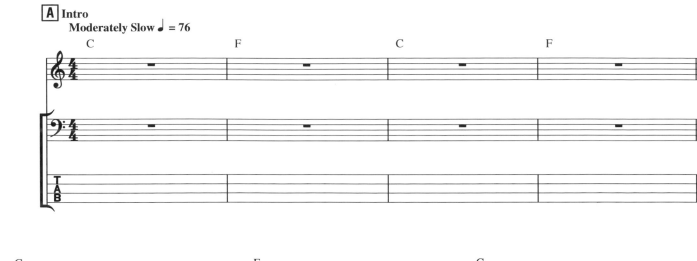

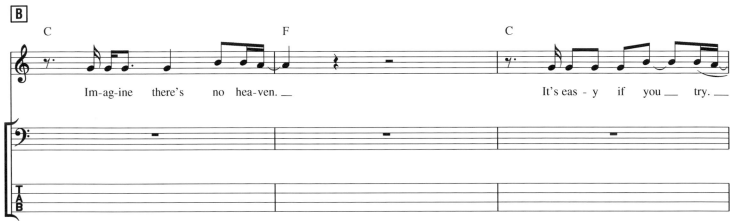

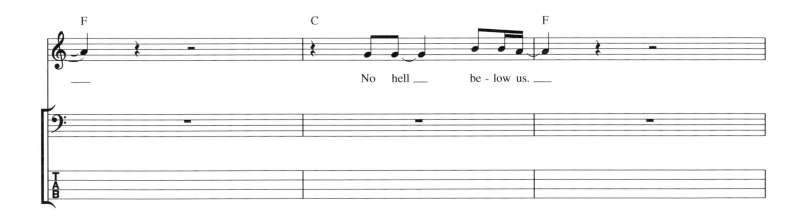

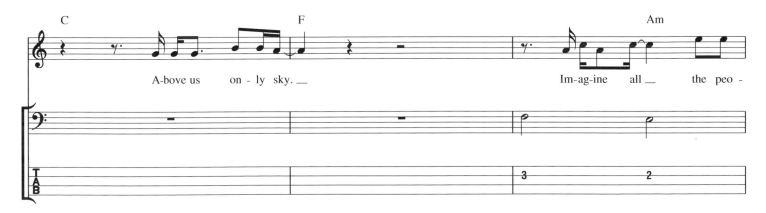

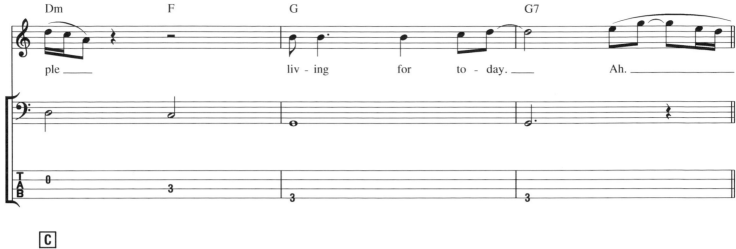

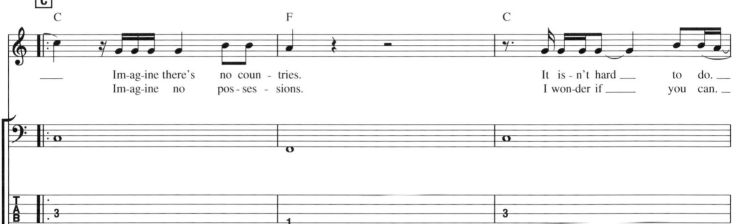

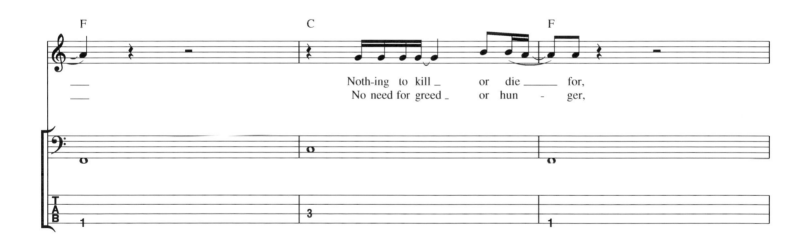

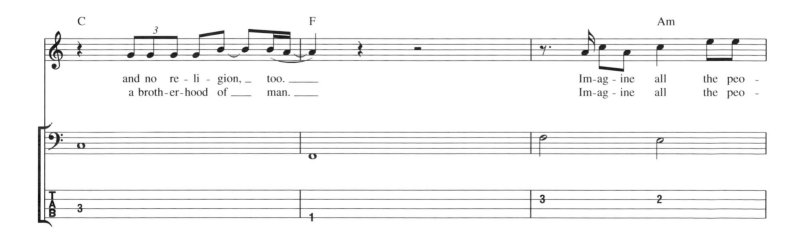

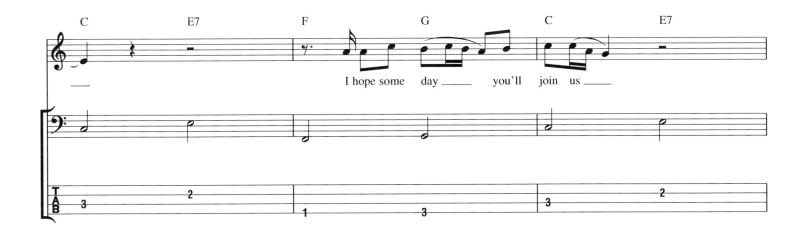

Layla

Words and Music by Eric Clapton and Jim Gordon

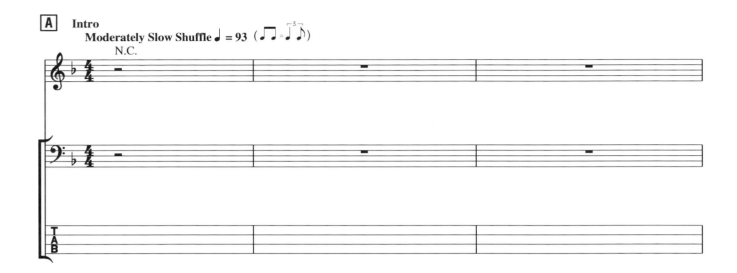

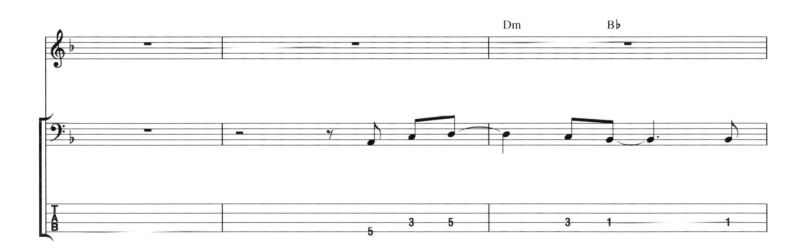

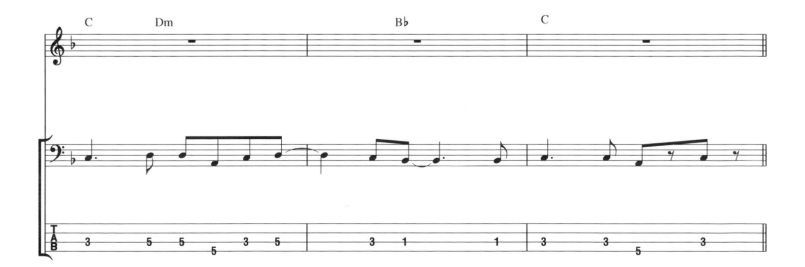

1. What _ will you do when you get lone - ly?   No - one wait-ing by your
2. Tried _____ to give you con-so-la - tion.   Your _ old man, he let you
3. Make _ the best of the sit - u - a - tion.   be - fore I fin - ally go in -

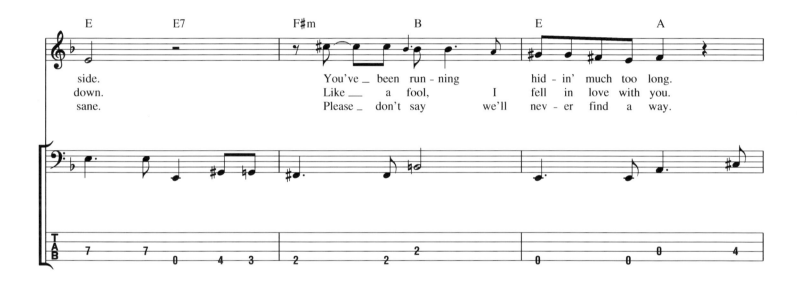

side.   You've _ been run - ning   hid - in' much too long.
down.   Like ___ a fool,   I   fell in love with you.
sane.   Please _ don't say   we'll   nev - er find a way.

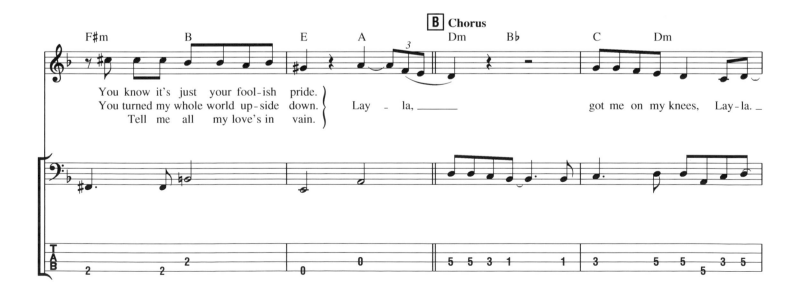

You know it's just your fool-ish   pride.
You turned my whole world up-side   down.   } Lay - la, _____   got me on my knees, Lay-la. _
Tell me all   my love's in   vain.

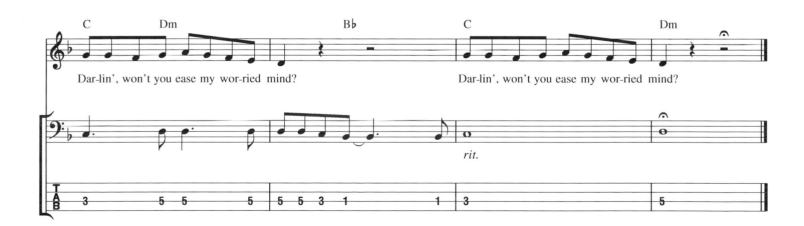

Maggie May

Words and Music by Rod Stewart and Martin Quittenton

No Particular Place to Go

Words and Music by Chuck Berry

go.
go.
belt.

Rid-in' a-long in my au-to-mo-

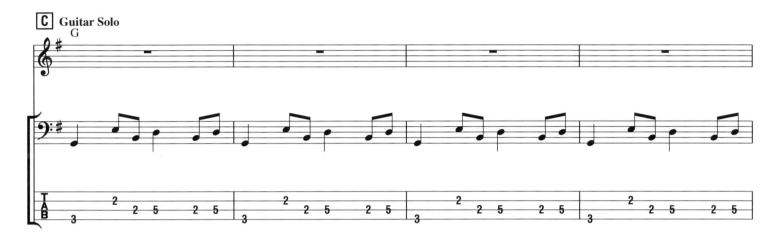

C Guitar Solo

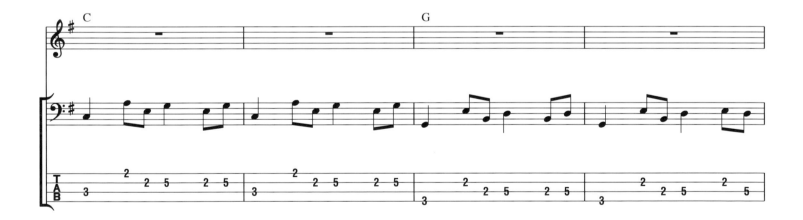

No par-ti-cu-lar place to

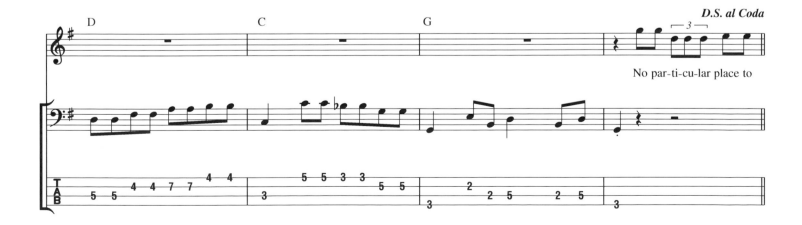

Takin' Care of Business

Words and Music by Randy Bachman

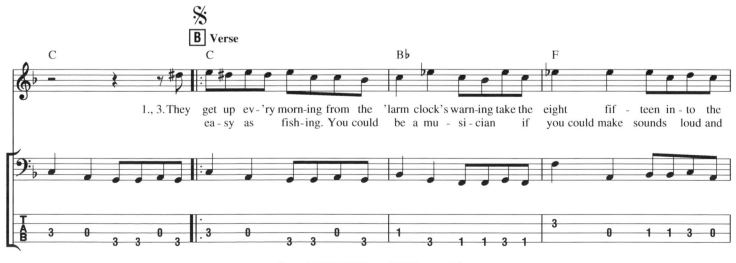

1., 3. They get up ev-'ry morn-ing from the 'larm clock's warn-ing take the eight fif-teen in-to the

ea-sy as fish-ing. You could be a mu-si-cian if you could make sounds loud and

cit - y. There's a whis-tle up a-bove and peo-ple push-ing peo-ple shov-ing and the girls who try to look pret -
mel-low. Get a se-cond hand gui-tar. Chan-ces are you'll go far if you get in with the right bunch of fel -

ty. And if your train's on time you can get to work by nine and start your slav-ing job to get your
lows. Peo-ple see you hav-ing fun just a - ly-ing in the sun. Tell them that you like it this way. _

pay. _ If you ev - er get an-noyed, look at me I'm self em-ployed. I love to work at noth-ing all day. _
_ It's the work that we a - void and we're all self em-ployed. We love to work at noth-ing all day. _

C Chorus

_ And I've been tak-ing care of busi - ness, ev-'ry day. _ Tak -
_ And we've been tak-ing care of busi - ness, ev-'ry day. _ Tak -

care _ of my busi - ness. When I'm a-way ev -'ry - day. __

F **Guitar Solo**

D.S. al Coda

C   Bb   F

3. They

⊕ *Coda*

G **Breakdown**

C   N.C.

Tak -

- ing care of busi - ness.   Woo!   Tak - ing care of busi - ness.   Tak -

H **Outro-Chorus**

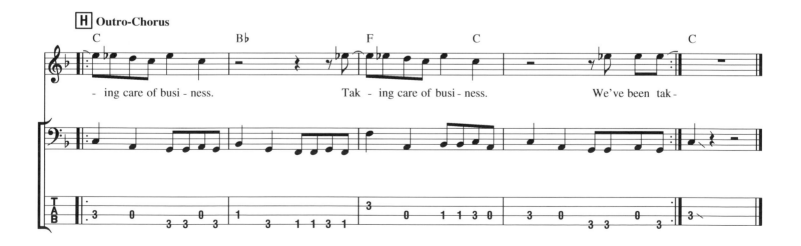

FastTrack MUSIC INSTRUCTION

*Fast*Track is the fastest way for beginners to learn to play the instrument they just bought. *Fast*Track is different from other method books: we've made our book/audio packs user-friendly with plenty of cool songs that make it easy and fun for players to teach themselves. Plus, the last section of the *Fast*Track books have the same songs so that students can form a band and jam together. Songbooks for Guitar, Bass, Keyboard and Drums are all compatible, and feature eight songs including hits such as Wild Thing • Twist and Shout • Layla • Born to Be Wild • and more! All packs include great play-along audio with a professional-sounding back-up band.

FAST*TRACK* GUITAR

For Electric or Acoustic Guitar – or both!
by Blake Neely & Jeff Schroedl
Book/Audio Packs

Teaches music notation, tablature, full chords and power chords, riffs, licks, scales, and rock and blues styles. Method Book 1 includes 73 songs and examples.

LEVEL 1
00697282	Method Book	$7.99
00697287	Songbook 1	$12.95
00695343	Songbook 2	$12.99
00696438	Rock Songbook 1	$12.99
00696057	DVD	$7.99

LEVEL 2
00697286	Method Book	$9.99
00697296	Songbook 1	$12.95
00695344	Songbook 2	$12.95

CHORDS & SCALES
00697291	9" x 12"	$10.99
00696588	Spanish Edition	$9.99

FAST*TRACK* BASS

by Blake Neely & Jeff Schroedl
Book/Audio Packs

Everything you need to know about playing the bass, including music notation, tablature, riffs, licks, scales, syncopation, and rock and blues styles. Method Book 1 includes 75 songs and examples.

LEVEL 1
00697284	Method Book	$7.99
00697289	Songbook 1	$12.95
00695368	Songbook 2	$12.95
00696440	Rock Songbook 1	$12.99
00696058	DVD	$7.99

LEVEL 2
00697294	Method Book	$9.99
00697298	Songbook 1	$12.99
00695369	Songbook 2	$12.95

FAST*TRACK* KEYBOARD

For Electric Keyboard, Synthesizer, or Piano
by Blake Neely & Gary Meisner
Book/Audio Packs

Learn how to play that piano today! With this book you'll learn music notation, chords, riffs, licks, scales, syncopation, and rock and blues styles. Method Book 1 includes over 87 songs and examples.

LEVEL 1
00697283	Method Book	$7.99
00697288	Songbook 1	$12.95
00695366	Songbook 2	$12.95
00696439	Rock Songbook 1	$12.99
00696060	DVD	$7.99
00695594	Spanish Edition	$7.99

LEVEL 2
00697293	Method Book	$9.95
00697297	Songbook 1	$12.95

CHORDS & SCALES
00697292	9" x 12"	$9.99

FAST*TRACK* DRUM

by Blake Neely & Rick Mattingly
Book/Audio Packs

With this book, you'll learn music notation, riffs and licks, syncopation, rock, blues and funk styles, and improvisation. Method Book 1 includes over 75 songs and examples.

LEVEL 1
00697285	Method Book	$7.99
00697290	Songbook 1	$12.99
00695367	Songbook 2	$12.95
00696441	Rock Songbook 1	$12.99

LEVEL 2
00697295	Method Book	$9.99
00697299	Songbook 1	$12.95
00695371	Songbook 2	$12.95
00696059	DVD	$7.99

FAST*TRACK* SAXOPHONE

by Blake Neely
Book/Audio Packs

With this book, you'll learn music notation; riffs, scales, keys; syncopation; rock and blues styles; and more. Includes 72 songs and examples.

LEVEL 1
00695241	Method Book	$7.95
00695409	Songbook	$12.95
00696657	Spanish Edition	$7.99

FAST*TRACK* HARMONICA

by Blake Neely & Doug Downing
Book/Audio Packs

These books cover all you need to learn C Diatonic harmonica, including: music notation • singles notes and chords • riffs, licks & scales • syncopation • rock and blues styles. Method Book 1 includes over 70 songs and examples.

LEVEL 1
00695407	Method Book	$7.99
00695574	Songbook	$12.99

LEVEL 2
00695889	Method Book	$9.95
00695891	Songbook	$12.99

FAST*TRACK* LEAD SINGER

by Blake Neely
Book/Audio Packs

Everything you need to be a great singer, including: how to read music, microphone tips, warm-up exercises, ear training, syncopation, and more. Method Book 1 includes 80 songs and examples.

LEVEL 1
00695408	Method Book	$7.99
00695410	Songbook	$12.95
00696589	Spanish Edition	$7.99

LEVEL 2
00695890	Method Book	$9.95
00695892	Songbook 1	$12.95

FOR MORE INFORMATION, SEE YOUR LOCAL MUSIC DEALER, OR WRITE TO:

HAL•LEONARD® CORPORATION
7777 W. BLUEMOUND RD. P.O. BOX 13819 MILWAUKEE, WI 53213

Visit Hal Leonard online at **www.halleonard.com**

Prices, contents, and availability subject to change without notice. Some products may not be available outside the U.S.A.

1015

HAL•LEONARD® BASS PLAY-ALONG

The Bass Play-Along™ Series will help you play your favorite songs quickly and easily! Just follow the tab, listen to the audio to hear how the bass should sound, and then play-along using the separate backing tracks. The melody and lyrics are also included in the book in case you want to sing, or to simply help you follow along. The audio files are enhanced so you can adjust the recording to any tempo without changing pitch!

1. Rock
00699674 Book/Online Audio $16.99

2. R&B
00699675 Book/Online Audio $15.99

3. Pop/Rock
00699677 Book/Online Audio $16.99

4. '90s Rock
00699677 Book/Online Audio $16.99

5. Funk
00699680 Book/Online Audio $16.99

6. Classic Rock
00699678 Book/Online Audio $17.99

8. Punk Rock
00699813 Book/CD Pack $12.95

9. Blues
00699817 Book/Online Audio $16.99

10. Jimi Hendrix – Smash Hits
00699815 Book/Online Audio......................$17.99

11. Country
00699818 Book/CD Pack $12.95

12. Punk Classics
00699814 Book/CD Pack $12.99

13. The Beatles
00275504 Book/Online Audio $16.99

14. Modern Rock
00699821 Book/CD Pack $14.99

15. Mainstream Rock
00699822 Book/CD Pack $14.99

16. '80s Metal
00699825 Book/CD Pack $16.99

17. Pop Metal
00699826 Book/CD Pack $14.99

18. Blues Rock
00699828 Book/CD Pack $16.99

19. Steely Dan
00700203 Book/Online Audio $16.99

20. The Police
00700270 Book/Online Audio $19.99

21. Metallica: 1983-1988
00234338 Book/Online Audio $19.99

22. Metallica: 1991-2016
00234339 Book/Online Audio $19.99

**23. Pink Floyd –
Dark Side of The Moon**
00700847 Book/Online Audio $15.99

24. Weezer
00700960 Book/CD Pack $14.99

25. Nirvana
00701047 Book/Online Audio $17.99

26. Black Sabbath
00701180 Book/Online Audio $16.99

27. Kiss
00701181 Book/Online Audio $16.99

28. The Who
00701182 Book/Online Audio $19.99

29. Eric Clapton
00701183 Book/Online Audio $15.99

30. Early Rock
00701184 Book/CD Pack $15.99

31. The 1970s
00701185 Book/CD Pack $14.99

32. Cover Band Hits
00211598 Book/Online Audio $16.99

33. Christmas Hits
00701197 Book/CD Pack $12.99

34. Easy Songs
00701480 Book/Online Audio $16.99

35. Bob Marley
00701702 Book/Online Audio $17.99

36. Aerosmith
00701886 Book/CD Pack...........................$14.99

37. Modern Worship
00701920 Book/Online Audio $17.99

38. Avenged Sevenfold
00702386 Book/CD Pack $16.99

39. Queen
00702387 Book/Online Audio $16.99

40. AC/DC
14041594 Book/Online Audio $16.99

41. U2
00702582 Book/Online Audio $16.99

42. Red Hot Chili Peppers
00702991 Book/Online Audio $19.99

43. Paul McCartney
00703079 Book/Online Audio......................$17.99

44. Megadeth
00703080 Book/CD Pack...........................$16.99

45. Slipknot
00703201 Book/CD Pack $16.99

46. Best Bass Lines Ever
00103359 Book/Online Audio......................$19.99

47. Dream Theater
00111940 Book/Online Audio $24.99

48. James Brown
00117421 Book/CD Pack...........................$16.99

49. Eagles
00119936 Book/Online Audio......................$17.99

50. Jaco Pastorius
00128407 Book/Online Audio $17.99

51. Stevie Ray Vaughan
00146154 Book/CD Pack $16.99

52. Cream
00146159 Book/Online Audio $17.99

56. Bob Seger
00275503 Book/Online Audio $16.99

57. Iron Maiden
00278398 Book/Online Audio $17.99

58. Southern Rock
00278436 Book/Online Audio $17.99

HAL•LEONARD®

Visit Hal Leonard Online at **www.halleonard.com**